T0168657

WHERE CLOUDS ARE

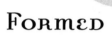

FORMED

THE UNIVERSITY OF ARIZONA PRESS   TUCSON

Where Clouds Are Formed

poems by Ofelia Zepeda

The University of Arizona Press

© 2008 Ofelia Zepeda

All rights reserved

www.uapress.arizona.edu

Library of Congress Cataloging-in-Publication Data
appear on the last printed page of this book.

Publication of this book is made possible in part by
the proceeds of a permanent endowment created
with the assistance of a Challenge Grant from the
National Endowment for the Humanities, a federal
agency.

Manufactured in the United States of America
on acid-free, archival-quality paper containing
a minimum of 30% post-consumer waste and
processed chlorine free.

contents

PART I

LOST PRAYERS

The Place Where Clouds Are Formed

I
Every day it is the same.
He comes home.
He tells her about it.
As he speaks, his breath condenses in front of his face.
She goes about her business;
every now and then she looks over.
She doesn't hear his voice.
She sees the soft fog that continues to form a halo.
She knows he is still talking about that place.
He never tires of it like she does.
Only on summer days when the air is hot
and moisture is still a long time in coming,
she asks him to tell her about that place.
She sits facing him.
Waiting for the first vocalic, non-stops,
the push of air from his lips.
He tells her of the place where clouds are formed.
The cool dampness of his voice is rich.
Even on a dry June day
her face beads with wetness
as he talks directly to her.
Each aspirated sound a gentle burst of coolness.
"Tell me again, tell me again," she teases.
If he knew she only wanted relief from the heat
and not the story, he would stop talking.

He begins, "The first time I saw the place
where clouds are formed was from
the window of a train . . ."
Another time was in a mirage
in the heat outside Tucson.
Once he thought he saw it
in the dry light of stars.
The place he remembers best
was when he saw it in the eyes
of a woman he spoke to.
When he first noticed it,
she hid it by lowering her gaze.
Soon she let him look freely.
There were times when she opened her eyes
wide, allowing an unobscured view.
Sometimes he saw her eyes smolder
with dryness on a summer day.
Other times she was rich with moisture.
Clouds came in succession.
The earth's shadows muted.
"You know the forty days
and forty nights?
I was there.
I'll be there when it happens again,"
she said with a slight smile.
Like a child, he rushed to look
into her eyes at every opportunity.
If he could, he would hang on her eye socket,
peering inside,
marveling at her displays.

II

An unusually cold December day right around Christmas;
clouds, mist find solace in the canyons of the Santa Catalina Mountains.
White moisture quietly moving amid the cactus.
Truly, clouds, wind, and rain are the few elements
that can touch the saguaro from head to foot.
Oblivious of spines, needles.
Rubbery hide surrounded, soothed by elements.
Contact triggers stored heat of remembered summers.
Moisture beads roll forward, unstoppable.
From the city below
we see mist rising, mist rising.

III

We sit close in the cab of the truck.
The weather is cold, wet outside.
Too messy to stand in
waiting for a school bus.
My father's truck is warm inside,
having been at work since four a.m.
The sound of the engine is soothing,
heater working to capacity.
Inside the cab we are silent.
We don't need language.
We listen to the regular hum of the engine,
rhythm of the windshield wipers,
soft rain on the hood.
Aware of the cold air
surrounding our temporary shelter.
We look out over the fields

where fog clings to the soil.
Every now and then
with the back of his gloved hand
he wipes the windshield.
"Is it coming yet?"
The three of us sit quietly,
breathing clouds.
Clouds condense as
they contact the coolness of the windows.
My father appears to breathe air
with temperature in balance.
He forms no clouds.
He watches us.
We continue to breathe
gray, soft mist, waiting for the school bus.

Trapped Air

Old ceilings ripped out.
Exposing rafters; beams;
dirt; old, compressed insulation;
electrical wires that go nowhere.
Heat from long ago summers.

The openings expose lost,
forgotten dreams that must have
gone there when the dreamer
turned his back for just a second.
These old ceilings are where
I imagine nightmares hide once a
mother comforts a crying child
disturbed by bad dreams.

Dust filters through the sunlight.
It settles on the sweat of a hot August day.
It sticks to the blood on the floor and wall,
an injury during construction.

At the end of the evolution of construction there is a
smooth, shiny glass-top stove.
The first time I cook on it, I realize I need to hold the handle of
the pot when I cook on this surface.
A one-armed woman cannot cook on this stove.

I watched the woman in the restaurant.
She has a full cast on her right arm.
Her breakfast arrives, pancakes.
Watching her, I realize eating pancakes is a two-handed job,
at least a right-handed one.
In her effort to eat, she manages to
knock over a glass of water.
After a while it is the little pitcher of syrup.
The waitress smiles at her with each cleanup.
Her husband comes over to her side of the table,
cuts a few slices of pancake for her just once,
as if showing her will make it easier.
After a while she gives up.

I imagine this woman having nightmares
brought on by her encased arm
and how it weighs on her in so many ways,
and by her hunger.
She has frustrating dreams of a pancake breakfast gone wrong.
Once she wakes from her nightmare,
bits of the bad dream collect in the dark corners
and crawl spaces of her house.

Crossing Mountains

I am ready.
My bundle, my power bundle,
hidden, but present.
My rosary is in the side pocket of my purse,
strung around sticks of gum,
the pen from the last hotel I stayed in.
The beads are poised to hail Mary.

Halls of the I.C.U.

My sisters are the first ones to arrive.
They designate their space.
The second group,
a Navajo family,
three women and two men.
The women are quiet.
The shuffle of their multi-pleated skirts
is the only sound.
There is a scent of cedar in their hair.
In this narrow space there is only room
for prayers and sorrow.
My sisters and the Navajo women
are aware of this.
Our brothers know it too and prefer to
stand at the edge of the space.
They stand with their legs spread, arms crossed,
poised for the sudden movement
of the earth in the wrong direction.
The Navajo men, on the other hand,
distract themselves momentarily.
They look into the waiting room,
a basketball game on T.V.
In the pleats of their skirts
the women hide sacred pollen,
leftover prayers, ways of beauty.
They carry it like contraband

to these sterile halls.
Smoke and mist from all-night prayers
keep the layers moist.
Female rains begin here.
Songs still echo in their skirts.
The Navajo women are quiet.
The shuffle of their multi-pleated skirts
is the only sound.

Birth Witness

My mother gave birth to me
in an old wooden row house
in the cotton fields.
She remembers it was windy.
Around one in the afternoon.
The tin roof rattled, a piece uplifted
from the wooden frame, quivered and flapped
as she gave birth.
She knew it was March.
A windy afternoon in the cotton fields of Arizona.

She also used to say I was baptized standing up.
"It doesn't count," the woman behind the glass window tells me,
"if you were not baptized the same year you were born,
   the baptismal certificate cannot be used to verify your birth."

"You need affidavits," she said.
"Your older siblings, you have some don't you?
They have to be old enough to have a memory
of your birth.
Can they vouch for you?"
Who was there to witness my birth?
Who was there with my mother?
Was it my big sister?
Would my mother have let a teenager watch her giving birth?
Was it my father?
I can imagine my father assisting her with her babies.

My aunts?
Who was there when I breathed my first breath?
Took in those dry particles from the cotton fields.
Who knew then that I would need witnesses of my birth?
The stars were there in the sky.
The wind was there.
The sun was there.
The pollen of spring was floating and sensed me being born.
They are silent witnesses.
They do not know of affidavits, they simply know.
"You need records," she said.
"Are there doctor's receipts from when you were a baby?
Didn't your parents have a family Bible, you know,
where births were recorded?
Were there letters?
Announcements of your birth?"

I don't bother to explain my parents are illiterate in the English language.
What I really want to tell her is they speak a language much too civil for writing.
It is a language useful for pulling memory from the depths of the earth.
It is useful for praying with the earth and sky.
It is useful for singing songs that pull down the clouds.
It is useful for calling rain.
It is useful for speeches and incantations
that pull sickness from the minds and bodies of believers.
It is a language too civil for writing.
It is too civil for writing minor things like my birth.
This is what I really want to tell her.
But I don't.
Instead I take the forms she hands me.
I begin to account for myself.

Aroma of Sorrow

She slides downward
against the wall.
Her body is no longer in control.
She shuffles as if shackled in weights.
In just minutes her sorrow increases tenfold.
She is like an aroma
triggering memories quickly.
She takes us back.
She takes us to a place we don't want to go.
We are anxious for her to pass, releasing us.
Her sorrow continues to fill
the room, heading for the exit.
Children on the floor
stop in mid-play and look up.

Lost Prayers

Passing below the sacred peak,
here prayers signified by rosary beads are futile.
Calling on the Virgin Mary is useless.

Instead, one must know the language of the land.
One must know the balance of the desert.
One must know how to pray
so that all elements of nature will fall into rhythm.
These are the kinds of prayers that will work.
Once uttered, the sacred mountains respond with coolness,
with gifts of wetness,
with gifts of civility of climate.

Empty plastic bottles are collected
from the desert floor,
replaced with ones filled with water.
In another location blue flags are raised in the desert,
signaling the location of water.
Signaling a chance for survival.
Flags recognizable by heat-demented minds.

The O'odham roamed the desert
with precarious steps.
Keeping an eye on the horizon, moving,
seemingly becoming a part of the heat and dryness
of their landscape.

They walk knowing the heat and aridity of their namesake place.
Never experiencing a mirage of running water,
swaying palms at a cooling oasis.
Never needing plastic bottles, flags to guide them
to water places.
They knew the trails leading to water.
They knew the natural water tanks
always with names like, Hodai Ṣon Wo'o, "Rock Pond."
These rock ponds later labeled "tinajas" on maps.

Labeled, the rock ponds offer no water sanctuary
for those crossing the desert unprepared.
Ironically, it may have been their distant ancestors
who put these water places on maps.
Instead, in the heat of the desert they rely on rosary beads
and calling on the Virgin Mary.

Ocotillo Memorial

Walking in the desert,
we come upon a memorial site.
Holy Family candle long melted.
Photograph of a young woman
with dangling earrings.
Her memory marked
by a stand of ocotillo.
In spring they will burst
red, orange blossoms.
Branches will bend forward.
Birds, insects will visit.
All around her are the Tucson Mountains.
Brown, mottled volcanic stones stand guard.
This string of mountains,
flight path for Tucson International Airport.
On approach the cabin becomes quiet.
Passengers buckle up.
Tray tables are stowed.
Seats are in upright position.
The plane flies low above the memorial site.
Acknowledging the woman with the dangling earrings.

PART II
OTHER WORLDS

Dirt

I
Lately I've been craving dirt.
I long to see how it
lies on freshly turned fields,
clinging to deep-digging equipment.
To see it, taste it.
I taste it through my nostrils
when dry dirt becomes wet
from a garden hose.
It is not enough.
I inhale, swallow.
Sympathetic sensory reactions.

Walking through a nursery
I am further drawn in the direction
of the center of the garden world,
potting soils, fertilizer.
Aroma intensified by the humidity of life,
strangely comforting.

II
Doing electrical wiring in our house
we bore holes into adobe walls;
rivers of dry dirt begin to flow.
The house is over thirty years old.
I knew the dirt was clean.

When opportunity arose,
I wet my finger,
lift the dirt, and put it on my tongue.
It tasted the way I thought it would.

A woman once told me,
"When we were children,
we sucked syrup from
ocotillo blossoms."
Syrup accessible only to hummingbirds,
bats. She said, "We gathered blossoms,
set them for the syrup to collect
in a little puddle in soft dirt.
Then we ate it.
It was just a little dirt.
It was clean dirt."
I know what she means by clean dirt.

III
Many think they know dirt, mud, and clay.
Potters, cement workers,
anyone claiming an occupation
with the stuff
don't know what children know.
Having spent an entire childhood
walking it unshod.
They know the hardness, smooth wetness.
Children know how unforgiving
it can be.
Making its way into shoes,

imbedding in unsuspecting fibers,
causing whites to go brown.
Forcing many mothers
who pride themselves on the
whiteness of their whites
to fall into despair
from which there is no recovery.

IV
Which one,
cold, hard dirt,
hot, hard dirt,
is worse for kneeling?
Mass celebrated outdoors.
Summer heat settles in
at ten a.m.
The faithful endure kneeling
and what seems like endless
minutes of standing.
Feet flattening into the dirt.
All before Vatican II.
Christmas Midnight Mass,
cold dirt floor of the Winter Solstice
is no friend of a child
having to endure the kneeling of the faithful.

Landscape

The early morning sounds are so clear.
Familiar in my memory.
The sound of boiling coffee.
The sound of shuffling feet, a step, a shuffle.
She didn't lift her feet when she walked.
She shuffled to her own rhythm.
Old wooden floors worn thin by her shuffling
and eight children.
She was short in stature.
Low to the ground.
She had joints that began
losing moisture and flexibility
when she first started to walk.
She didn't lift her feet.
She was in constant contact with the earth.
With each shuffle she pushed the earth along,
with each step she dragged time along.
She pushed bits of her past
and bits of her future
in uncertain amounts and
in uncertain directions.

Oig 'am si, 'oig 'am si	Come now, come now
Si g o 'e-keihi	Step lively
Si g o 'e-keihi	Step lively
Att o 'i-hudiñ g cewagĭ	We will pull down the clouds

Att o 'i-wai g ju:kĭ	We will call the rain
Oig 'am si, 'oig 'am si	Come now, come now
U:gk o himc g jeweḍ	We will make the dust rise
U:gk o himc g jeweḍ	We will make the dust rise
Att o 'i-hudiñ g cewagĭ	We will pull down the clouds

In awe I watch young men bound two,
sometimes three, steps at a time,
and young women as they virtually float
effortlessly across minor obstacles.
I, on the other hand, am a profiler.
I have no interest in ethnic distinctions.
Instead I survey with a biased eye
for uneven terrain before my journey.
I take special note of stairs, steps, tall curbs, grading.
I take note of minor ones,
breaks and seams of seemingly
smooth sidewalks,
roughness of asphalt and gravel walkways.
I consciously lift my foot with every step.
Unlike most, I am aware of the unevenness of landscape.
I know the earth has no smooth surfaces.
Primordial memories
store the memory of glacial movements
and carving of landscape.
I am aware of canyons reshaping themselves every moment.
Somehow I know water and air are not smooth
and molecules require speed bumps.
I am aware of strategically placed signs

for pedestrians of earth:
Hold onto handrails
Watch your step
Caution
Moving walkway will end
Please be prepared to step off
Keep shoelaces and straps away
from moving parts
Open-toed shoes not allowed
Please keep walkway clear.

The Other World

She said, "When we get back to
our world, can we rent a video
we can all watch?"
"What do you mean, our world?
This place is your world.
This place of sand, rocks, mesquite,
rattlesnakes, lizards, and little rain.
This is yours."
"Oh, okay, when we get back to the other
world, can we rent a video . . ."

A clear dry night in the Kofa Mountains,
where stars are visible even on the horizon.
We sit with heads tilted and marvel at them
all evening long.
At one point we watch a satellite watching us.
We point out the Milky Way in its dense gray majesty
resting quietly on a massive carpet of black.
They call it the backbone,
the universe's nervous system.
If the Milky Way falters in its rhythm,
it is a sign of our violation of the rules of civilization.
Some of us will look at each other and wonder
which ones, some will begin selling alibis,
and others will find temporary shelter
in the land down under.

Ñeñe'i Ha-ṣa:gid

Ha-ka: 'ac g ñeñei'i mo 'am kaidaghim
Am kaidaghim taṣ hudñig wui.
Am kaidaghim si'alig ta:gio.
Am kaidaghim ju:piñ ta:gio.
Am kaidaghim wakolim ta:gio.
Am 'ac ha'icug 'id ṣa:gid,
mo 'am kaidaghim.
S-ap ta:hadag 'o g t-i:bdag.
S-ape 'o g t-cegĭtodag.
S-ape 'o g t-jeweḍga.
S-ke:kaj 'o, ñia 'an g 'i-ñeid.
S-ju:jpig 'o, ñia 'an g 'i-ñeid.

Ka: 'ac g ka:cim ṣu:dagĭ t-miabĭ 'at.
Ka: 'ac g ge'e jegos t-miabĭ 'at.
Ka: 'ac g s-ke:g hewel t-miabĭ 'at.
Ka: 'ac g s-ke:g ñeñe'i t-miabĭ 'at.
Ka: 'ac g s-ke:g ñeñe'i t-ai 'at.

In the Midst of Songs

We hear the songs resounding.
They are resounding toward the sunset.
They are resounding toward the sunrise.
They are resounding toward the north.
They are resounding toward the south.
We are in the midst of songs.
Our heart is full of joy.
Our mind is good.
Our land is good.
The land is all beautiful, take a look.
There is light rain all around, take a look.

We hear the ocean in the distance.
It has come near us.
We hear the beautiful wind in the distance.
It has come near us.
We hear the dust storm in the distance.
It has come near us.
We hear a beautiful song in the distance.
It has come near us.
We hear a beautiful song in the distance.
It has come upon us.

Music Mountains

Cemamagĭ, Tumamoc
Babad Do'ag, Santa Catalina Mountains
Cuk Do'ag, Black Mountains, Tucson Mountains
Cew Do'ag, Rincon Mountains
Giho Do'ag, Kihotoa, Burden Basket Mountain
Waw Giwulig Do'ag, Baboquivari Mountain

It has been said before,
these mountains will not listen
if we simply speak words to them.
They will only hear us
if we come with melody, rhythm,
pitch, and harmony.
To these circling mountains
we must speak with voices
in songs, rhythmic speeches, orations, and prayers.
We must be prepared with repetition,
a singular, undisturbed beat.
That is the way of mountains.
This is what they want to hear.

We must come to them with music
so they are generous with the summer rains
that appear to start their journey from their peaks.
We must come to them with song
so they will be generous
with the winter snow that settles there.

We must come to them with a strong recognizable beat,
a beat that reaches the core of the mountain —
a core still molten and moving to its own sounds —
and simultaneously reaches
a core long frozen into submission
with only a memory of the heat of its birth.
For the mountains of Tucson
the sound of spoken word is not enough.
They will not hear us.
We must be prepared
with harmony,
a strong rhythm,
a beat.

Traces

Sitting in the desert on a Sunday morning
I make minor observations.
Resting my ankle on the opposite knee
I notice the skin there.
Fine lines running like minor tributaries.
like patterned cuts in a jigsaw puzzle.
The white, dry lines are clear against brown skin.
Flakes begin to peel away
making space for new.
With each movement more flakes fall.
A cycle that is a part of me, and all that claim skin.

I think back and find myself in a swimming pool
where I learned to swim at thirty-five.
I move in the water with reluctant grace.
On a backstroke I see the Space Shuttle
riding back to Florida.
Flakes of my skin in the water cleansed by chlorine.
Pieces of skin now a part of rubble and new cement.

I stand up.
With each step pieces of skin flutter downward,
caught momentarily on the inside of my pant leg.
I continue to walk.
Flakes fall onto the cuff of my sock.
Resting in what must seem like an eternity
for such a migration.

It falls and comes to a longer
rest on top of my shoe. It rides.
It rides the muddy current of the Colorado River,
finding places where the water is clear, green.
Part of me finds its way to
sediment at the bottom of that river.
I will be part of the disturbance
when rocks move again.
Reshaping a canyon.

It rides the water and mud to
the entry point at the ocean.
I move gracefully in weightlessness among ocean life.
My skin floats to the bottom of the floor.
I touch just enough seashells.

I continue walking.
In a dry wash I step on a hill of sand.
The piece of skin riding on my shoe falls.
At dusk a coyote wanders through the wash.
He picks up my scent.
It leads nowhere.

Wild Horse Pass Resort
GILA RIVER INDIAN RESERVATION

Moon setting on the Estrella Mountains.
Artificial waterways.
Rolling green hills.
Dew rests on the early morning light.
Winter dry mesquite, cottonwood trees on the banks.
Little brown ducks submerge and reappear.
Larger ones float by easily, one takes wing,
soft spray leads from wing to water.
Light floats around the corner.
Plastic lawn chairs line up.
Umbrellas hang like cocoons.
Early morning light spreads
across the Estrella Mountains.
Breezes shift.
Steam off a heated pool moves
across the cooler water of the lagoon.
Bear grass hugs the walkway.
A woman walks by smoking a cigarette.
She does not notice the moon setting on the Estrella Mountains.
Undulations of light on the green hills are interrupted.
A train of small maintenance vehicles.
Little brown ducks dunk heads into the water
on a cool February morning.
The moon is setting on the Estrella Mountains.
Sun rises, mist glistens on the golf course.
Young mesquite trees stand vigilant
over the grass, always a nursing plant.

Winter migratory birds wade on the water's edge.
Shoots of cattail enclose the playing brown ducks.
The moon sets on the Estrella Mountains.
Milky, white, light reflection, becoming pale.
It descends.
Sunlight brightens on the Estrella Mountains.

Sounds of Ceremony

The sound of jingle of bells.
The sharp scrape of seashell against shell.
The muffled shaking of butterfly cocoons.
The tiny stones from an anthill.
Rolling inside a gourd, round and round.
Dizzying.
Wood against wood of a rasp.
Hide against hide of a taut drum.
Wood against wind.
A bullroar.
A basket faced down in the dirt.
Reverberations.
Vibrations.
Caught by the air for its journey.
Other times held by the earth in her folds and creases.
And still other times riding on the wings of a hummingbird.

Tsegi Overlook

"Tsegi Overlook," menu item at the Junction Café.
Three scrambled eggs with jalapeño jelly.
Not meant for the weak of heart.
We have oatmeal and toast on this cold morning.

An O'odham in Yosemite

My O'odham world is turned upside down.
July, with temperatures etched in triple digits,
we head for California.
Yosemite, in July we wear jackets
and light sweet-smelling fires in our tents
each morning to take the edge of the cold off.
Deer wander on the edges of the camp area,
unafraid.
We stand in the parking lot watching them feed.
At the registration desk we leaf through the photo album.
With some anxiety we look at images of cars torn open
like cardboard boxes.
Broken windows, doors mangled as easily as a piece of paper.
We are warned about not keeping food in our vehicle
or our tent. They are serious when they talk about this.
We have no room to doubt them.
We attempt to be fastidious
and obediently utilize the bear boxes in the parking lots.

The grass here is thicker than that of green places I've known.
Thicker and greener than northern Arizona.
The White Mountains cannot compete.
Is it the elevation, the snow level?
The kind of rain they must get here.
Something in the water.
We take a walk.

Passing a sign designating the famous John Muir Trail.
Trees with red snow markers
ten feet, fifteen feet up. Unfathomable.
We sit on the grassy bank,
put our feet into the icy cold water of the Merced River.
I lie back on this sunny Yosemite morning.
Watch white thunderclouds begin to gather.
It is quiet and perfect for a mountain morning.

In the evening the crunching sound of footgear on
gravel paths across Tuolumne Meadow.
At one point a voice says, "Turn off the flashlights."
We all instinctively hit off switches.
It's a moonless, cloudless night.
We stand in the meadow and look up.
To an outsider we must have looked like a group of animals
frozen in fear, or perhaps we resembled early
people who in their first wanderings stop
to observe something never observed before by humans.
With our shared senses and knowledge of our world
we look around. The stars are thick above the granite peaks.
The dome of stars is a white mass above us.
We look all around in awe. Awe, broken
by someone slapping a mosquito.
Otherwise, it is a quiet and perfect mountain evening.

PART III

How to End a Season

Proclamation

Cuk Ṣon is a story.
Tucson is a linguistic alternative.
The story is in the many languages
still heard in this place of
Black Mountains.
They are in the echo of lost, forgotten languages
heard here even before the people arrived.

The true story of this place
recalls people walking
deserts all their lives and
continuing today, if only
in their dreams.
The true story is ringing
in their footsteps in a
place so quiet, they can hear
their blood moving
through their veins.
Their stories give shape to the
mountains encircling this place.
Wa:k is the story of
water memories of this desert.

Citizens gravitate to Sabino Canyon.
The humming, buzzing, clicking of water life,
the miracle of desert streams
on smooth boulders.

Rocks, sediment older than life itself
serve as reminders.
It should be unnecessary for sticky notes
to remind us what a desert place is.
A place dependent on rains of summer,
light dusting of snow,
the rarity of dry beds as rebel rivers.
It is real desert people who lift their faces
upward with the first signs of moisture.
They know how to inhale properly.
Recognizing the aroma of creosote in the distance.
Relieved the cycle is beginning again.
These people are to be commended.

It is others who lament the heat of
a June day, simultaneously
finding pride on surviving
the heat — a dry heat.
These individuals should simply
be tolerated.

Opposed to those who move
from one air-conditioned environment
to another, never acknowledging the heat of summer.
Being grateful for November, when
temperatures drop below eighty,
complaining of the lack of seasons in the desert,
heading for mountains
to see colors —
these people — well, what can we say.

We must feel for the dogs of Tucson.
Who bark as if they belong to somebody and
who, before the rain, wish they were a color other than black.

Wa:k is the O'odham place name making reference to natural water sources.
Wa:k is also the place for San Xavier del Bac, located near Tucson.

How to End a Season

Food is put in place for the ancestors.
Prayer sticks are buried for the saguaro, for the season, for the earth.
Songs are sung for the spiritual health of everyone, everything.
In the fading light of a bright summer day
the people sit down to eat and visit.

There are decorations paying commercial homage to the saguaro.
Balloons with smiling little saguaros on them,
and others in large type reading SAGUARO, and in small letters, "Credit Union."
Amid the festive decorations, the sun lowers on the horizon.
Colors begin to show.

The people are treated to stews of chile,
different types of beans, tortillas, and breads.
Salad and chicken for the kids.
And of course there is the ever-present *ciolim* for everyone.
Marigold, lavender, and a touch of hibiscus
hang above the dry desert mountains.

The singers' voices carry songs across the desert floor.
To the east a bright star takes a long trailing fall,
the glow is wide and slow.
The people point.
The *gohimeli* songs begin.
They step to the rhythm, feel the beat of the earth.
They look at all that is around them

and drink the wine for the goodness of the earth.
As the celebration continues,
a toy-like machine stumbles across the landscape of a red planet.
NASA knocks on the window of America's childhood memories
with "Rover," "Yogi," and "Barnacle Bill."

JULY 16, 1997

NOTES: Saguaro Credit Union was once an active credit union in Tucson. *Ciolim* is a bud from the cholla cactus harvested in spring by the O'odham; it is dried and stored for year-round use as a vegetable. *Gohimeli* is a dance step from O'odham traditional ceremony. In 1997 planet Earth received images from Mars.

Mogollon Rim

That light that we shared
left us that day.
I don't know how it left, I just know it did.
I have gone searching for it.
I look around the rim of this edge of the world and wonder.
Did it leave on the wing of a hawk?
The one I saw riding the current on the rim
of the canyon, sweeping in and out of the shadows.
Did it leave with the sudden rush of wind in the upper pines?
Did it leave with the seeds of the cones that came falling,
landing on rock, never finding roots?
Did it leave with the swift heat that passed through the forest
on tips of flames during the summer fires?
Did it get buried in the charred ruin of timber?
Washed away in swift, uncharted tributaries of rain.

That must be how it left us that day on the Mogollon Rim.
When it left, I cried. I cried into the corner of the tent where I lay.
I cried when the wind was loudest that night.
My crying could not compete with a summer storm;
instead I used it as my camouflage.
Wind, swaying and rushing of pines,
clattering of our tent — my pain was silenced.
The hurt was hidden that night.
My tears fell on the plastic floor of the tent.
I pushed them into the corner so no one would see.

The tent will be folded up tomorrow.
The corners will be pulled tight, dusted off.
It will be folded from corner to corner, military style,
put into its carrying sleeve and original box.
Once back in Tucson it will go to the storage shed.
The last camping trip of the summer.
My pain, emptiness from that one night, will be put in storage.
Forgotten until next summer.

Hopi Blue

The heat has been too strong.
You are no longer able to stand tall.
Energy is more difficult to produce.
Chlorophyll eludes you.
Photosynthesis is only a fond memory.
Supplements don't help.
Stems are brittle, they crackle and splinter
with each movement.
Face is downcast, masked with a paper sack,
harvesting your bounty of seeds
promising your legacy.
When the sack is removed,
your days are spent watching ants make their way up
and down again, pulling the last nutrients.
Bees no longer visit.
Lush, sweet pollen has been spent in youth.
Leaves the size of elephant ears quietly
drop to the ground with a strong breeze.
A large disfigured shadow of yourself.
Bright yellow petals now only exist in
a digital picture they took at your peak.
You were so beautiful then.

Squash Under the Bed

There was always crooked-neck squash under our beds.
The space under the bed met the criteria of a cool, dark, dry place.
These large, hard-skinned squash with speckled, serrated,
green and yellow designs shared space under our beds
with new cowboy boots, lost socks, forgotten toys,
dust, and little spiders.
The squash rested under there with our memory of summer.
Awaiting winter darkness.
With the cold weather, we split the hard skin and expose the
rich yellow meat inside, the bounty of large seeds entangled
in the wetness of their origin.
We saved the seeds for next summer.
We eat the soft, sweet meat of the winter squash.
We swallow the warmth of summer.

The Way to Leave Your Illness

If you have an illness that won't go away,
take a journey.
When you get there, leave it.
Place it on a rock; throw it into moving water;
bury it. Throw it into the wind.
Let it go.
Leave it there for others.
She had been sick for many days.
In her frustration she remembered
what her grandmother used to say,
"Take it far away and leave it there."
She walked to the other end of campus
toward the library.
In her mind she left the discomfort, ache, pain, there.
She walked back, comforted,
knowing she didn't bring it back with her.
Her illness is now hidden in the stacks.
Perhaps it is temporarily in periodicals.
Or archived in Special Collections,
or perhaps in fiction, no longer real.

Just Like Home

The young woman buys
a piece of fresh fry bread from
the Indian Parent Association's booth.
"Oh, just like home," she says.
"Do you have any salt?"
I pour a small amount in her palm.
She sprinkles it on her bread.
She takes a bite, "Mmm, just like home."
She seems unaware she has her eyes closed
as she eats and talks.
The delicate bite of freshly cooked bread
takes her back.
She stands on a street in downtown Tucson
and thinks of women so familiar to her,
her mother, her sisters cooking outside.
In the distance the sound of someone
chopping wood, a barking dog.
Piñon smoke is so real for her right now,
her hair might smell of it if she moved
and the breeze caught her just right.

Words on Your Tongue

You come here on silver wings.
You gather on a fruit-ripening month.
You come from the river people.
You come from the people of the foothills of
the Sierra Nevada.
You come from the people of the tall pine.
You come from the people of the round earth place.
From the four corners of the earth.
You come with the glint of turquoise in your eyes
and salt on your tongue.

    You come here and see a lost sandhill crane
     sitting on top of a telephone pole in the desert.
    You watch him survey the land for moisture.
    Moisture still a long time in coming.
    You watch as his attention is momentarily
     distracted by empty washes and the memory of wetness.
    You hear him cry the word for water.

You come here on silver wings.
You come from the people of the towering clans,
from people of desert lands,
from ones where rivers cross.
You come from people who are water bearers.

You come with pollen resting on your shoulders
and the smoke from cleansing blessings

still lingering in your clothes.
Your family blessed you before you traveled.
They had prayers for your safety.
They held out gifts for you,
gifts of words, of stories.
You come to us from people with
words on their tongue.

Road Man's Son

The Peyote Road Man's son sings a song for me.
He closes his eyes.
Pulls words, melody from his mind.
His body is in the room with me
but he is outside.
Where songs must be.
Where spirits must be.
He sings for the Peyote Spirit on a school day.
He is the Road Man's son.

Do'ag Weco

Ia 'ac gegok do'ag weco
kc 'an 'u:gk ha'icu ñeid.

We stand below the mountain and look upward.
We look upward in humility, in prayer.
From the tops of mountains come memories
of stories, songs, names of plants,
animals we have long forgotten.

Old people dream of days they walked
mountains paths.
They dream of their sturdy step,
lack of fear of a desolate mountaintop.
They see things there only rendered in song.
Lower parts of mountains are for all humans.
We walk along a mountainside knowing
ancestors' bones sit in the mountains.
They watch us as we pass. We are not afraid.

On an unusually cool July day we drive to Waw Giwulig.
Arriving at the foot of the mountain
I place a towel on the damp bench and sit down.
This place is green and moist.
The air is blue.
Light mist drifts, swayed by breezes.
For a few hours on a summer day
this mountain is in tune with the wet side of ocean islands.

Ia 'ac daḍhă do'ag weco kc 'an 'u:gk ha'icu ñeid.
We sit here below the mountain and look upward.

Ia 'ac daḍhă kc t-ho'igeid.
Tt amjeḍ hab t-ju: mo hab a wua g O'odham
c am ha'icu ta:ñ g t-na:toikam.
T hab masma 'ab 'i-hi: 'i:da t-taccudag
mat hab masma o i-hi: g wi'inam ṣu:dagĭ.
Ñia'a.

Gewkdag 'att 'am tai.
Duakag 'att 'am tai.
Apedag 'att 'am tai.
Att amjeḍ 'am 'ep 'i-da:mc c hab hahawa 'ep cei.
Gewkdag 'att 'am m-tai att hab masma s-ap 'in o 'oyopod
c 'an o 'i-ha-we:mtad hegam mo pi 'eḍgid g gewkdag.
S-duakag 'att 'am m-tai 'att hab masma
s-ap 'in o 'oyopod c o s-he:kigk.
S-apedag 'att 'am m-tai 'att hab masma
s-ap 'in 'o 'oyopod c s-ape wuḍ 'o O'odhamk.

Ia 'ac daḍhă do'ag weco kc 'an 'u:gk ha'icu ñeid.
We sit here below the mountain and look upward.

Before we do anything else, we open
our voices to a greater being.
We say we are grateful for being allowed
to be here in this wonder.
And like flooding water, the requests for gifts begin.
We ask for strength.

We ask for health.
We ask for goodness.
Finally we feel we need to justify
our requests; we begin again.
We ask for strength to complete the things
we have started to do with our lives.
We ask for health so that we may walk
with a sturdy step,
with good breath,
and clean light in our eyes.
We ask for goodness so that we may have open minds,
open hearts.
We ask for patience to deal with all those who require it,
and pass it on to those who are impatient.
We ask for forgiveness so we can forgive those who require it,
and pass it on to those who are unforgiving.

Ia 'ac daḍhă do'ag weco kc 'an 'u:gk ha'icu ñeid.
We sit here below the mountain and look upward.

Waw Giwulig is the most sacred mountain for the Tohono O'odham.

Calling on Ancestors

The Navajo poet reads.
He stands under the mesquite tree at night
in imagined shade.
He calls on his clan members.
Those who are no longer here.
He calls on those who may wander
these deserts, walking paths of old Athabascans
who headed for points north thousands of years ago.
He calls on their memories,
encouraging them to
come out of the shadows of dry washes.
Asking them to leave the
the companionship of the Huhugam.
He reads his poems as the branches of
the mesquite tree rustle.
On that night they come in the form of
a nice summer breeze.

Huhugam means "those who are gone, disappeared"; they are the ancestors of the O'odham.
Literature typically spells this term "Hohokam."

Outside Payson

The blur of snow in the shadows.
Edges tinted red.
A black bird sits.
He dreams in contrasts of black and white.
The driver ahead of us
brakes for a cow in the road.
We pause in our minds.
Farther up we catch a deer in our headlights;
it crosses our minds.
We roll by at seventy-five miles an hour.
Anticipating the lights of Chinle.

Sunset

She hurriedly rushes by.
We turn our heads,
catch a glimpse
of a multi-colored skirt
disappearing beyond the horizon.
Red, orange, yellow, toxic pink,
finally a glint of white.

Pain of Speaking

I hear them laughing.
A joke.
I have no clue.
In my grandmother's mind a million
pieces of information
I cannot access, at least not yet.
I bought a book for learning the language.
I hear them talking.
Sometimes just by the rhythm
I know they are talking about me.
Right in front of me!
Having no voice in this language
makes me invisible.
It hurts.
I scream!
They look at me.
Guilty.

Walking with Language

Some have carried it, held it close, protected.
Others have pulled it along like a reluctant child.
Still others have waved it like a flag, a signal to others.
And some have filled it with rage
and dare others to come close.
And there are those who find their language
a burdensome shackle.
They continually pick at the lock.

Blacktop

The blacktop carries me
    Past Three Points.
    The security of the homelands passes by me.
It carries me past San Pedro where weavers
    Sit under the watto.
    Their voices drift into
    The tangle of desert where all language goes.
The blacktop carries me
    Into the tohono,
    Into the heat,
    Making me delirious.
    San Lucy sounds like a country western song.
The blacktop carries me
    In all directions.
    Sometimes I am traveling with a lone eagle.
    Other times I roam with worse scavengers.
    The blood on the heat of the blacktop
    Calls me.
    It calls me as if it has always known my name.
Anonymity is my desire.
    Walking instead in sandy washes and rocky hills unseen,
    Leaving the debris of my life under a mesquite tree,
    I rush toward an imaginary new life.
The blacktop carries me in all directions.
    It knows my name.
    I never told it my name.
    It calls me.

It wants to carry me in all directions.
    It whispers, "You will always see Waw Giwulik
                                In your rearview mirror."

Redefining Home

A home is both the spaces inside and outside the building.
A home is more than just the structure, the house, ki:,
the hogan, wikieup.
Ki: in O'odham means both "house" and "home."
It is the aroma, the textures of the building that help us remember.
The smell of the wet dirt walls,
the smell of dry dust.
It is the smell of the green brush on the roof, in the walls.
It is the texture.
The smooth mud walls,
the rough ribs from cactus and ocotillo,
the branches of cottonwood and posts from cedar and pine.
Home is a place that has the right feel,
the right smell,
the right sense of coolness when you touch the walls.

Watto/Ramada

Am watto weco, 'am watto hugidan.
Beneath the ramada, next to the ramada.
Things happen there.
Meals are cooked there.
Meals are shared there.
Good news is delivered there.
Bad news is delivered there.
People laugh there.
People cry there.
People mourn their dead there.
People celebrate births there.
A multi-purpose place.
Watto, ramada,
A family gathering place.
An outdoor kitchen.
An outdoor sleeping area.
A roof for shade, no walls.
The sun goes by overhead, oblivious
to what is beneath the watto.
The moon goes by overhead, but beneath
the watto all things remain in shadow.
Under the watto, in the quiet shade of darkness,
the people gather to do the things they must do.
The watto is only for people and things they must do.

Seeing Red

Red is the color that calls the moisture.
Drop the skin of the fruit and be sure it
is facing up,
be sure it is visible to
all that is in sight.

With the longest wavelength in the spectrum
visible to anyone, anything with eyes.
Red reaches out.
The color arouses energy, passion, and aggression.
Everyone knows this.
The red of the skin
is the signal to the entities
who seek this color.
Female rain begins to gently move and
male rain is distracted from his dreams by the color red.

Science claims animals don't see colors
or only see two; red is one of them.
Coyote knows this and with his fill
turns the skin facing up.
Ants know this and, upon gorging, leave enough red.
Packrat knows this and landscapes his yard with
the skin of the red fruit.
Dove is the first one to feast
but cannot concern herself with this practice.
It is meant for everyone else.

Aligning Our World

It is important to wake facing east.
Facing the sunrise,
The origin of the day,
The direction you pray.

A conference in Dallas.
A hotel room not in line with the east.
My roommate looks around,
"Which way is east? You have no mountains
So I can't tell."
A young black man, the bellhop,
Points in the direction he knows as east.
"Can we move our beds? We must wake facing east,"
She asks.
He shrugs and begins to help us align our world.
We push beds, dressers, nightstands, and lamps.
We push the moon, the stars, and the earth.
Like the tumblers in a combination lock, we
Hear them roll, we can feel the anticipation of the
Right set of numbers, click, click.
The earth's axis makes this sound as we continue
Moving furniture.
The stars screech and scratch the sky —
A sound one wouldn't expect from stars.
I have heard this sound before when
Stars wake me from sound sleep with their movement.

The loudest is when one falls.
We hear that final familiar click when everything
Falls into its rightful place.
The young man starts for the door.
"We'll put it all back when we leave,"
We shout as he walks out the door.

Smoke in Our Hair

The scent of burning wood holds
the strongest memory.
Mesquite, cedar, piñon, juniper,
all are distinct.
Mesquite is dry desert air and mild winter.
Cedar and piñon are colder places.
Winter air in our hair is pulled away,
and scent of smoke settles in its place.
We walk around the rest of the day
with the aroma resting on our shoulders.
The sweet smell holds the strongest memory.
We stand around the fire.
The sound of the crackle of wood and spark
is ephemeral.
Smoke, like memories, permeates our hair,
our clothing, our layers of skin.
The smoke travels deep
to the seat of memory.
We walk away from the fire;
no matter how far we walk,
we carry this scent with us.
New York City, France, Germany —
we catch the scent of burning wood;
we are brought home.

Ofelia Zepeda is a member of the Tohono O'odham Nation of southern Arizona and was born and raised in Stanfield, Arizona. She is a Regents' Professor of linguistics and recipient of the MacArthur Fellowship for her work in American Indian language education, maintenance, and recovery.

She has published works in the Tohono O'odham language and in English. Ofelia Zepeda has two books of poetry, *Ocean Power: Poems from the Desert* and *Jewed̦ I-hoi/Earth Movements*, and is the co-editor of *Home Places*, a celebration of twenty years of publication of the Sun Tracks series, and of *Home: Native People in the Southwest*. Her poetry has also appeared in numerous anthologies and journals, including *Reinventing the Enemy's Language*, edited by Joy Harjo and Gloria Bird; *Fever Dreams*, edited by Leilani Wright and James Cervantes; *Poetry of the West: A Columbia Anthology*, edited by Alison Deming; and *A Narrative Compass: Women's Scholarly Writing Journeys*, edited by Betsy Hearne and Roberta S. Trite. Her poems also appear in the permanent exhibit "Home: Native People in the Southwest" at the Heard Museum in Phoenix. Dr. Zepeda is the series editor of the University of Arizona Press's Sun Tracks Native American book series.

Ofelia Zepeda's areas of teaching and research include the introduction to the Tohono O'odham language, the structure of Tohono O'odham, issues of language documentation and revitalization, and Native American literature. She published the first grammar textbook of O'odham, *A Tohono O'odham Grammar*. Her scholarship includes numerous published articles on the status of Native American languages, language policy and planning, and Native American linguistics and education. She is a co-founder and director of the American Indian Language Development Institute (AILDI), one of the longest running indigenous-language institutes with an international reputation for training educators of Native American students.

Library of Congress Cataloging-in-Publication Data

Zepeda, Ofelia.

  Where clouds are formed : poems / by Ofelia Zepeda.

    p. cm. — (Sun track series ; v. 63)

   ISBN 978-0-8165-2778-6 (acid-free paper) —

   ISBN 978-0-8165-2779-3 (pbk. : acid-free paper)

  1. Sonoran Desert—Poetry. 2. Indians of North
America—Arizona—Poetry. 3. Tohono O'odham
Indians—Poetry. 4. Deserts—Arizona—Poetry.
I. Title.

PS3576.E64W47   2008

811'.54—dc22   2008018866